Poems for a Tranquil Mind

Ashley H. T. Barnsley

Neon Crocus Books

First published in Great Britain in January 2001
by Neon Crocus Books

Text Copyright 2001 Ashley H. T. Barnsley
Photograph Copyright 2001 Ashley H. T. Barnsley

ISBN: 0-9538213-1-5

Printed and bound in Great Britain by
FM Repro Ltd, 69 Lumb Lane, Roberttown
Liversedge, West Yorkshire WF15 7NB

'Tranquillity is the key'

About the author

Ashley H. T. Barnsley

Born in Wakefield, West Yorkshire, England in 1958,
Ashley H. T. Barnsley quickly realised his poetic
disposition. He made early entries in the *'Modern Poets'*
collection and went on to co-author *'Suppositions: Poems
for the abstract and the inebriate'*.

'Poems for a Tranquil Mind' is *Ashley H. T. Barnsley's*
most comprehensive anthology to date, spanning nearly
three decades of writings. Created from the hypothetical
and the experiential, its variant pathway firmly ignores the
parameter-stuck bastions of the ordinary and makes no
apology for the author's uniqueness as a poet.

Contents

Foreword xi

Poems
Timepiece 1
Intrusion 2
Exist 3
That's it (Pedantic) 4
Sanctuary of Sleep 5
Beauty Cloaked 6
Demise of a Rose 7
Never the Same 8
Snakes 9
From You 10
Ice 11
Swans 12
No Smoking in Heaven 13
You 14
Someone Said 15
The Warlock 16
Swimming in God's Pond 17
Sarcophagus 18
She's Terrific 19
Understand 20
If the Dead are Watching 21
Forsaken 22
Should you tell your Babies? 23
Privilege 24
Bruised Cross 25
About Love 26
Enthusiasm 27
His Wife likes Him 28
Calm Sea 29
Gentle Death 31
Bite 32
Darker Side (As I feel now) 33
Quell the Tide 34
Tomorrow 35
Shell 36

Voyages of Obsession 37
Bed 38
Not Tidying up 39
Design a Body 40
Cacti 41
The Angel on Golden Wings 42
Still Some Life 43
Paces 44
Dash 45
Pod 46
Shadow of the Giant Tree 47
Chilled 48
Food 49
Suppose 50
Unsavoury 51
Last Stop Dies 53
I Wrote this 54
Stopping 55
Red 56
Introsurdity 57
Parting (Maybe) 58
Proud 59
Too Many 60
Strange 61
Immovable 62
Obviously Important 63
Reckless 64
Here 65
Two Kids 66
Treadmill 67
The Beast Devours 68
Perfect Heart 69
Half-a-Sleep 70
Visitor 71
Folk 72
Looking Back 73
Sleeping 74
Push him over (Don't) 75
Consideration 76
Again 77

Mending 78
Tender 79
Ticking Over 80
Slightly Smiling 81
Harder to Write 82
It's no Fun being a Pet 83
The Mind a Tome 84
True Friends 85
To be Free 86
Think of Me 87
Illumination 88
6 am 89
Sorting 91
On Physical Beauty in People 92
Historic 93
Rescue 94
And then Sleeps 95
Laying 96
Outside 97
Undignified 98
For the Bottle 99
Emulation of the Egg-man 100
Flesh-Hunter 101
Living with Submission 102
Calculating 103
Fields 104
These Solitary Tones 105
Devotion to Cats 106
Enfolding 107
Addiction 108
Some Day, We'll just be photographs 109
Drink This 110
Tranquil Mind (A broken lock) 111
Crazed 112
Hearts and Flowers (Ending on a good note) . . . 113

Notes for readers 115

Chronology 117

The author's quotes 119

Foreword

Poetry is fluid, it has no boundaries, take a pen and write what you like, that's my philosophy. I know the great poets and masters of romantic verse are a cultural and influential tour-de-force, but it doesn't mean poetry is entrenched by their presence, it can't be. The poems in this book are a fusion of varying poetic dimensions and offer a liberating expression of writings. They are not held back by any preconceived notions of what the poetic rules are, because there aren't any.

'Poems for a Tranquil Mind' is a view from outside the peripheral fence, an incomparable poetic experience and an unchartered journey that hacks an analytical and thought-provoking trail through the very undergrowth of what we see and what we do. A journey which only you the reader can make and one from which only you can return.

'Poetry manifests from a lifetime of hopeless humility'.
 – The author.

Timepiece

Feel the time ticking away
Relentless day by day,
Watch the clock unable to
Rearrange, accepting change.
Feel the river move beneath and
Touch the soles of the feet,
Let the wind embrace, and let
The snow and let the sleet.
Observe the furrows of the skin,
Experience it change within.
Bow to the wrinkled brow
And somehow
Feel the breeze and feel the mist
And feel the sea and the foam
And if you can't rearrange the timepiece
Let the sea and the clock hands alone.

Intrusion

Rush of sound,
A fountain's catharsis
Exploding amongst Lilies.
The sheen of surface calm
Taunted by a cannonade
Of clear water.
The pool warmed,
Tastes the sunlight glints
And hosts the myriads
Of manic life forms
Emerging in the natural order
Of this microcosm.

Surrounded with plants
Eagerly looking from the edge,
The theatre of fish
Perform daily under
A pale blue firmament.
Created from nature's
Prodigious palate,
This government of order
Repels intrusion.
But would intrusion
Be from Mother nature's enemy
Or from Mother nature's Son?
Or are both the same
And be done?

Exist

Life is not perfect,
Nothing is.
If you seek perfection
You are beginning
A journey of despair,
A journey of frustration.
Perfection eludes,
Don't try to find it.
It does not exist.

That's it
(Pedantic)

I am so pedantic
It's hard to live my life
All the details have to be perfect
Although mistakes are apparently rife.
So it can all go and shit,
Everything's imperfect
Including me
– that's it.

Sanctuary of Sleep

Wandering at night
As you lay in your bed,
A thousand thoughts
For you to dread,
Or unrequited loves
And spine tingles that
Seep from the head.
Do you pretend you'll never end,
As an immortal
With a body not yet to send
To hell or heaven's gates?
Lay you down softly now,
Inside the mind to hum,
Taste this tranquil place
And await
A longer sleep to come.

Beauty Cloaked

One for sorrow
More for superstition,
But birds are no enemy.
Magpies look at you out of
The corner of their eyes,
Rip your black bags.
One for sorrow
Two for some fornication
We never see.
Magpies have to live.
One for sorrow
One for pinching litter.
Beauty cloaked in treachery
Misconceived, missing the point.
Demon is the rifle
Not the Magpie,
He only goes about his
Usual business.
His shiny feathers,
One for sorrow,
Two in the air – stuck up at you.

Demise of a Rose

Covet thee not for
Sensations from the
Warmth of a heart,
It is not you to exist here
With soul now torn apart.
Like the demise of a Rose,
Lost love must now lie,
But be born again to
Unprecedented kiss,
For from the Roses' thorns
This time is not for you to die
And to realise
For you now is this.

Never the Same

In hospital, having
Tonsils out,
I was just a lad,
The trauma of
Maternal separation,
Made me
Feel really bad.
After it was all over,
I would always
Maintain,
The body had
Fully recovered
But the head was
Never the same.

Snakes

Since the garden,
There has been no pardon
From God or man,
From inception,
There has been no affection
For the ophidian.
With this burden the herp lies low,
Striking back a blow,
When he can, if he can.
Interwound in the cruel
Machine of nature,
The creature,
All-carnivorous in sheets of muscle,
Dripping with power,
Will devour,
Will strike back at the stigma
With reptilian force.
The genus,
Coiling and constricting,
Has to eat the furry ones,
– the ones who people love
And show affection.
The curse of the
Creeping one unabates.
Forced-fed with austerity,
Persecution remains,
And again the serpent strikes back.

From You

From both were I
And from you to the
Physical world did I emerge.
Not always manifest
Were tranquillity and the calm.
Many times on your shoulder I cried,
Responses always were yours,
But inadequate sometimes were mine.
Self-qualities in I are questioned
And fade the comparison to yours.
Through the ages we have loved
And lost but never to weaken.
Love and bond can never be replaced,
In gratitude I remain always.

Ice

Amidst the ice of my life,
The cut and thrust of everyday strife,
Stands a whirlwind of emotional fears,
A heart full of unused tears.

Swans

Uncertain he is,
Although people tell him
He is a person on earth,
Why he sees Swans when
His eyes are closed.
He is curious, this is
An endless plight.
He lives tormented by
Existence, he may die with
No answers, still he can
See Swans.
He signs not his life away
And he fights no wars,
He knows,
Swans exist on sacred
Streams, along with saints
And whores.

No Smoking in Heaven

Don't be greedy
With this little weedy,
Take your time for sure.
He's your friend
But he's your foe,
What you'll reap
He used to sow.
Take all your drags
Not too deep,
Stub your tabs
Crossed fingers keep.
Listen carefully now
You're well,
There's no smoking in heaven
But there may just be in hell.

You

You can't do anything
With the past,
Except from it learn,
And you can't change
What will be
No matter how you yearn.

Someone Said . . .

Someone said you had left early
From this mortal place, without a sign,
They said you did your own hours
And were never a slave to the time.

Someone said you had left early
Probably laughing, that wasn't rare,
There's no clock card that says goodbye
And there's an empty feel in the air.

Someone said you had left early
Your mystery never to lack,
This time they're saying with sadness
. . . they don't think you'll ever come back.

The Warlock

The Warlock waits to
End the story,
Never can he turn his
Head from drink,
But under his dirty coat
Lies not a fickle word.
He told of hate and truth,
He told of war and death,
He drinks four gallons of beer
A day and sixteen gills of meths,
        . . . life has taken his smile.

Swimming in God's Pond

You looked good
But maybe didn't mean much,
You swam well
But maybe weren't that important.
You were a fine example
In the confines of your abode,
Did our lack of understanding
Cause you to overload?
You had no superstar status
Only water and some rock,
Outside your sphere was laughter
From those with intent to mock.
When the curtain came down on your show,
You had been living fast, but then died slow.
If suffering brings us closer to our maker,
Guess now, you'll be swimming in God's pond.

Sarcophagus

Within towers of silence,
The flesh-eating vault lies soundless,
Partial to the putrefying meat.
This stone box holds cataleptic spirits.

Carved in hieroglyphics,
Sleeping Kings levitate to the after life,
Lowly subordinate slaves stay encased.

Catalogues of embalmed souls
From tangible skulls and bandage,
Exist within the pyramidal sphere.
On cold marble slabs they are found
Whispering, under the dankness of a
                    buried eternity.

Silent, the sarcophagus is entombed history.
Those in slumber lie therein with treasures,
. . . and the ancient Egyptian Jackal-headed
                    Gods of the dead.

She's Terrific

She's a whiz
And she's a dream,
She can Hoover and
Do the washing machine.
She pairs socks
And irons the shirts,
She cooks dinner
And never seems to hurt.
She looks after children
And cleans window panes
She feeds the pets,
Never goes insane.
She's terrific, she's fab,
She's got something
I've never had.
She's also got a part-time job
And most of her spare time
          is robbed.
She's got muster
And she's got vigour,
And why I have not
I just can't figure.
Still in all this toil
And all this work,
A sign of cracking
Never lurks
And in all this work
Without a fee,
In all this crisis,
She's still got time
For me.
Then I turned around
and sighed,
That last bit . . . I lied.

19

Understand

You've one of
These in your head,
Some very dense,
They look pretty
Menacing
But make a lot
Of sense.
Pirates have them
On their flags,
Tattoos on arms sell,
Labels on old poison bottles
Display this sign as well.
It's a home for
The brain,
A cavity for the
Organ grand,
The inside bit you
Definitely need
If this poem
You are to
Understand.

If the Dead are Watching

If the dead are watching
We'd better carefully tread,
We'd better cover up our bodies
And not romp around the bed.

If the dead can read our thoughts
We'd better go with care,
We'd better not think the things
That with others we don't share.

If the dead are listening
We'd better carefully fare,
We'd better not be vulgar
Or curse or damn or swear.

If the dead are watching
Caution is not to spurn,
We'll all have to be good people
Until the watching is our turn.

Forsaken

Why forsaken?
– The bird,
– The fish,
– The burdened beast.
What provision is
Made in the holy books
For their gentle souls?
Does your God forsake them
Because of their easy submission?
If your God says it is granted
    to kill and exploit,
        – look into their eyes
        and tell them
           . . . God is love.

Should you tell your Babies?

Should you tell your babies to be good babies anymore?
When you yourself on being good are not without a flaw.
Should you tell your babies where morals they should find?
When you yourself on morals cannot make up your mind.
Should you tell your babies to find honesty and be true?
When you yourself don't stick but deviate from these two.

Should you tell your babies how to play attack and not defence?
When you yourself prefer to watch sitting on the fence.
Should you tell your babies which vice they should rebuff?
When you yourself are habit formed and can't give up the stuff.
Should you tell your babies how to be fit and alert?
When you yourself have eluded these in favour of the inert.

Should you tell your babies not to use words obscene?
When you yourself whisper words with expletives in-between.
Should you tell your babies to be leaders amongst the pack?
When you yourself choose your seat nearer to the back.
Should you tell your babies to find education and be refined?
When you yourself found little and from refinery declined.

Don't let your babies read this themselves among,
Because then they will know your hypocrisy and still not
                    what's right or wrong.

Privilege

I never realised how close
We were until he left,
I never realised his absence
Would leave a heart bereft.

An uncommon pact of
Snake and man,
A privilege did I behold,
From me he
Left for a better place
And comforted I am to know.

('Kane' left for Flamingoland Zoo
  on 2nd April 2000).

Bruised Cross

Can we meet you when we die?
Can we be friends?
We never gave up on you as an idol,
We never swore your name.
Amidst the confusion and the
Modern world, we never lost sight
Of you, although you faded in parts.
A figment or a truth
We know not, but hope we find.
You wouldn't smoke in latter-day,
You wouldn't drink
And be over indulgent.
You wouldn't eat meat
Or agree with vivisection.
Gentle of animals and children
And tortured by the mortal,
You can tell if good or
Wickedness prevails in the soul.
Potentially our last memory
Is of a bruised cross,
History or myth.
Don't forget us if your entity
Is material.
The needy wonder if you elude.
You are the forgiving lamb
And you we yearn to hold.

About Love

All this killing,
All this fear and nervousness,
All this dominance and submission.
The weak falling to the strong.
Dogs eating Dogs.

Nature, surely God did not create.
He's all about love, not killing.
Is he not?

Enthusiasm

Never been that keen on sport,
Maybe a little when I was a lad,
I was in the school Rugby team
But the enthusiast was really my Dad.

He was well into Rugby
And hoped I would be the same,
But I couldn't live up to his expectations
And didn't like playing the game.

He watched at every touch-line
For his son to get hold of the ball,
But only seldom did this happen all season
– from me there was little at all.

Other kids would sometimes remind me
That as a player I should be aware
– I wouldn't have even got near the team
Had my Dad not have been there.

We ended up as school champions,
We held the cup for all to see,
But in terms of team contribution
My Dad gave it much more than me.

His Wife likes Him

His wife likes him a bit
But hates his drunken ways,
She likes him best on medication
Drugged and in a daze.

Calm Sea

The man said . . . don't bring me back
              this way no more,
I won't be tempted by the sunset
              or moved by a moonlit shore.
I prefer to stay there when I am gone
              rather not be back in any form.
Don't bring me back this way no more,
I won't be seduced by Bluebells
              or miss the stars . . . I am sure.
Let me lie down like calm sea
              not be troubled by all this,
              let me go . . . let me be.

Gentle Death

Gentle death,
Upon when shall I feel thy
Kiss on my brow?
Seek sanctuary in the yards
And I will meet thee there when
I have parted from my life.
I would wish upon our rendezvous
That you will carry an answer,
Wear it under your cloak, let no
One see it lest they have gone
Before.
Let me find a truth within your
Arms and in return submit my flesh
For your awaiting grasp.
I listen for your call – you will
Find me a breath away from birth
And death alike.
Gentle death, thy kiss can
Not be as sour as life who has
Before you gone.

Bite

I've no solution
To the problems
That people hold,
I've no problems
To fit the solutions
That to me are often told.
I've no answers or questions
Or any other quip,
So suck on this
Or kiss an arse
Or go and bite
On your lip.

Darker Side
(As I feel now)

As I feel now,
I can't imagine life
Without strong Lager
Holding me devout
To its shining light
And to its cause,
Being worthy
Of my great applause,
Being worthy
Of my absolute
Attention and I can't refute,
That while it's very good,
I can confide,
– I know it has a darker side.

Quell the Tide

Looking in a mirror,
Parts have fallen away,
Others have changed
Texture and colour.
Once dealt the fervour
Of youth, the man fights
Here to maintain
The status quo,
Like swimming against
The force of a whirlpool.
A victim of changing biology,
– struggling with the brain.
If questions are from the core,
Do they tell of under value?
A strength can rear its head
But may tell of worthlessness.
Meanwhile – try to
Quell the tide.

Tomorrow

Tomorrow I will stop all this,
Stop drinking cans of beer,
I'll indulge only once a week
And wait for the mind to clear.

Tomorrow I will stop all this,
I'll not light up anymore,
I'll pack in the demon cigs
Even though I've failed before.

Tomorrow I will stop all this
And get a thinner form,
Probably take a little exercise
Instead of laying down.

Tomorrow I will stop all this
And see it finally done,
Tomorrow I will conquer all
. . . unless tomorrow never comes.

Shell

His shell is as hard as hell
But his insides are a quiver,
If life's a ship on an ocean
He's a canoe on a river.

Voyages of Obsession

Have you turned the light off
And have you checked the fire,
Have you locked all the doors
And laid submissive to this desire?

Have you examined your life-plan
And fulfilled your long term aims,
Has the itinerary of daily tasks
Been achieved without self-blame?

Does a button left out of its tin
Seem like a major threat,
Do the items not yet put away
Hang like an unpaid debt?

Do you categorise your belongings
With chronology and precision,
Does the weight of what needs doing
Spawn anger and cloud vision?

All this trivia to organise
A million things to think,
Daily voyages of obsession
. . . may make the vessel sink.

Bed

His wife is no drinker,
She thinks the over-indulgence is a crime,
But if she could drink more like him
They would do it all the time.

Drinking,
Pour it in the head,
Smoke some cigs and get Rat-arsed
And then make the floor a bed.

Not Tidying up

I am to stop
Tidying up afterwards,
There is no point
To it I know,
It will only be the same
Again shortly,
And for the trouble
There'll be nothing to show.
They don't care,
– like the others, they
Are having fun,
Rightly this is the case,
They couldn't care less
About any mess
And will willingly
Laugh in your face.
They sneer and poke
Fun at the rules,
Scant albeit they've been,
But in the depth
Of frustration
With some realisation,
– as children
We're all like it, it seems.

Design a Body

Design a body,
Missing off the crud,
Make it more streamlined
Make it look bloody good.
Don't include silly bits
That make stupid sounds,
Be careful with each orifice,
Give it confidence abound.
Design a body,
Make it look bloody good,
Bodies like this design,
Have them we all should.

Cacti

Prickly bastard.
Why should I be a pin cushion?
When I look at you I feel
The depth of your colour.
Smooth green as a backdrop
Weapons spiked and ready.
Spikes are for revenge,
If you miss-water
It does not die,
The Cactus lives
And laughs at you.

The Angel on Golden Wings

We help each other,
I help you and you help I,
When you are shot from the skies
By bitter thoughts and cruel deeds,
I pull the arrows from your tattered
Wings and repair your wounds
With droplets of devotion.
Sometimes I wonder where you are,
Especially in a time of need.
I look to the streams
And the pools of rain water for your
Reflection and see nothing,
Then you turn up as an image
In the tears of the mortal reflected.
The angel on golden wings,
You are my unknown mirror,
Forever we will float
On the calm waters of our freedom.

Still Some Life

There's still some life left yet,
A few more beers and maybe a cigarette.
A deliberation and a scratch of the head,
Over indulgence and some time in bed,
But there's still some life left yet.

There's not much energy to be found
And still pills and capsules lying around.
Just a micron of beauty with the beast
And not much dancing at the feast,
But there's still some life left yet.

Still a few meagre hairs on the dome
A place where skin feels more at home,
And maybe poison in the chalice
And still no King at the palace,
But there's still some life left yet.

Still room for pseudo-pleasure
And a little watered down leisure,
A growing indifference
And a developing resilience
And still some life left yet.

Still life in this old dog,
Still some vision in the fog.
A resistance to falling apart,
Maybe a stone will cushion the heart
And there's still some life left yet.

Paces

Sorry for the self-penned
Bastardisation
– the one from the bard,
I think maybe you are right,
Living with these idiosyncrasies
Could be only a couple of
Paces from
Hard.

Dash

Don't know what I'm
Writing about this time,
I've put fingers to the keypad
But no thoughts are in the mind.
I am tapping away at the keys
Like an enthusiastic writer,
But in doing this I still don't feel
Inspiration or much brighter.
I am still stuck what to write about,
Nothing created or to amend,
In fact I can't think of anything,
So dash it – that's the end.

Pod

Inside his pod
Life's a little strange,
It's an emotional vacuum
For a drunken sod
And a place that has been arranged.
This bubble is detached and remote,
One where his life shuts him in,
But at least it's warmer inside
Because the outside is as frosty as sin.
Sometimes the outside allures him
With a pretence of comforts so near,
Then on feeling the tools of rejection
He chooses to get back in his sphere.

Shadow of the Giant Tree

Large and sprawling
Muscular and contrived,
Home to the flighted animal,
A bedrock for nature.
You are the very foundation
Of this world.
You hold us in your arms
Caressing our skin
With your strong
And textured wood.
When you are gone,
We will have expired
Beforehand
And be in your
Shadow for all time.

Chilled

If you try to be self-righteous
And try to be confident and chilled,
There'll always be someone to remind you
That you can never be self-fulfilled.

Food

The older you get
The younger other people appear,
The crisp foundations of others' youth
Remind you of your own decaying years.
But they shouldn't get too excited
At this fit and fresh stage,
What's young and strong today
Is food to be ravaged by age.

Suppose

Anybody can write poetry,
It's not major intelligent stuff,
Anybody – but they might
purport just enough
To make out it's a big deal.
But we won't squeal,
Anything can be called prose,
Anybody can write poetry,
We more than suppose.

Unsavoury

If the Birds and Bees
Makes you displeased
And the Kama Sutra
Puts you ill at ease,
If human contact is
Not your kick,
And gyrating bodies
Not your hobby,
Don't curl up your lip.
Bear a thought
Without retort,
Realise, be clear,
Without this most
Unsavoury act,
You wouldn't even
Be here.

Last Stop Dies

Ignorance has no defence
And on a bus searching for kicks,
Minds expanded,
Chemistry altered,
Cold reality put you in the dark.
Who's behind the skin and bone?
The disorders?
The elastic thoughts?
Innocent people have it easy.
Lightning paranoia reflecting in
A window on a bus.
The youthful,
The drug,
The breakdown,
Halt this bus,
Last Stop Dies.

I Wrote this

I wrote this without thinking,
I wrote this on a whim,
I wrote this with no meaning
And without the lights being dim.
I wrote this unpaid, without a focus,
I wrote this without a lark,
I wrote this on the spur of the moment,
I wrote this without the dark.
I wrote this without chewing nails
Or cradling my head,
I wrote this without being over-sad
Or wishing I was dead.
I wrote this without 'ciggies'
And without being drunk or daft,
I wrote this very uninspired
It never made me laugh.
I wrote this at speed
Without much grey matter,
I wrote this without a care,
I think I've nearly finished now
   . . . so I think I'll leave it there.

Stopping

This rare feeling of sobriety
Makes him feel quite good,
He thinks he may stop drinking,
Just like his wife said he should.

Recklessness is to go
And hangovers won't exist,
He's only to keep off the stuff,
He's only to resist.

He'll strip down the layers
And present himself as clear,
– but he's stopping writing this
Because it's reminding him of beer.

Red

Inebriation,
Not a colour blue,
Vascular crimson
Tinges,
Burgundy toning hue.
Dilation,
Capillary dousing scheme,
Saturated ambience
Addictive type of theme.

Introsurdity

A thin divide,
Subtle, intense,
Introsurdity,
Which side of the fence?
Mind over matter,
Does it matter if you don't mind
Who's as mad as a hatter,
The blank page will be lined.
Looking like metal bars
If the page you should turn,
But the words will all fall,
– can't read them or learn.
Introsurdity,
Neurones not firing in calmness,
But not hurting, being harmless.
Let's all have a beer,
Let's all have a drink,
Let's sit down and have a think.
A thin divide
And now I swear,
Introsurdly calm
But don't give a fuck and
Sometimes aware,
Of a condition not in a book.
Introsurdity, this-is-what-I-bear.

Parting
(Maybe)

Maybe I am saying goodbye,
Dear friend and confidante,
Gatherer of my dreams,
Maybe I am saying goodbye to
Your perception changing themes.
Maybe gone, the icy feeling
That rests upon the tongue,
Maybe gone the stream of
Amber pure,
– a crutch to lean upon.
Maybe I am saying goodbye,
This comes from the heart,
Because I know being with you,
Is maybe worse
Than being apart.

Proud

If you're a bully
You'll swat flies,
Laughing as they
Dive downwards
From the skies,
With sad compound eyes
And little vapour trails.
It's like a sky scraper
Swatting men,
Giant against the tiny,
So then, don't feel good
It's hardly a match,
Don't feel good
About your catch.
When you kill and
Victory claim aloud,
You must realise
Killing in any form
Is never anything
To be proud.

Too Many

There's too many people in this world,
Six billion and rising,
There's too many people on this earth,
Being born faster than dying.
There's too many people in this world,
Makes you feel small,
I often think if there were only ten,
I would know them all.
There's too many people in this world,
I'm a grain of sand,
There's too many people on this earth,
It's getting out of hand.
There's too many people in this world,
Something is very wrong,
There's too many people in this world,
. . . maybe it'll be better when we're gone.

Strange

When we're old
We'll look back
And think
About our life.
We'll try to think of
Someone who liked
Our strange spirits
Or even our
Ability to drink.
We'll hope we were
Not just a tiny part
In a great multitude.
We'll hope we could
Have been important
– if only to ourselves.

Immovable

The body can be a tool
In a war of attrition.
The naked animalistic flesh
Used on the front line.
The muted marital state
Resting uneasy
Between fights and verbal
Onslaughts.
But it's time to recall the tanks
And the army,
Defeat and the white flag.
To the victor
A submission,
A prisoner of contact,
A prisoner of the feminine entity
And all its immovable power.

Obviously Important

Snakes might strike at you
Or if they're big enough
They might try to consume you,
But,
They won't nick your money
Or let you down.
They won't deny you marital comforts
Or try to stop you drinking.
They won't mess with your car
Or talk behind your back.
Snakes are obviously important.
People,
There's billions of people,
Most of them ugly
But Snakes,
They are beauteous and
Have dignity and integrity.
Those who would scorn the Snake
Ought to feel it the other way around.
Some people can't stand beauty.

Reckless

This is the
Alter ego,
A saturated
Stumbling
Coping mechanism.
This is the
Megalomaniac.
This is the arm
Pumping visionary.
A delivery of
Self-indulgent,
Fake-tattooed,
Alcohol-ridden
Cig-tainted
Bastardism.
The inducer
Of hangovers.
The reckless
Totality.

Here

I am not to judge
What you have done,
I am not to give chase
When you decided to run.
I am not to scent the blood
That pumps within your head,
I am not to lick your soul
When you have before me bled.
But I am here to watch over you
If you should ever need,
I am here with ample strength
If on this you should ever feed.
To you I am no stranger,
Not another you will see,
To you I exist much closer,
Look in the mirror – that's where I'll be.

Two Kids

One says yes
The other no,
One stays at home
The other wants to go.
Disharmony yes,
Tranquillity not,
One of them wants
What the other's now got.
One wants this way,
The other one that,
One stands up,
The other one's sat.
'I like my hair shorter',
'I like it long',
Both of them right,
Neither one wrong.
'I painted a house'
'And I a train',
'Which one's best?'
– 'We like them
Both the same'.

Two kids squabble,
Won't make amends,
But in the
Passage of time
They'll soon be friends.
(They are sisters).

Treadmill

Scraping the beans from a tin,
Soiled nail beds and beard thin.
Cider swilling in print huts,
Hard liquor with callous looks,
Misery when the supply shuts.
Expect a giro, beg a smoke,
Dodge a refuge, wait to croak.
Never of fixed abode,
The psychotic overload
Walks the treadmill in bitter cold.
Maybe summer will bring hope
And bring a bar of soap,
But maybe the vagrant
Won't give a thread
If he's here or if he's dead.

The Beast Devours

The stinging salt of food part eaten
Lies on chewed fingertips,
Hands that grip the fruits of money
Throw the items at the face.
The primeval mechanism
Of the orifice devours
In some bizarre biological act.

Inherent in the body of the beast
Is the need to consume until over-full.
Eagerness swallows the rewards
Before being fully chewed,
Using hyper-mandible movements and
Over zealous use of the tongue.

Perfect Heart

Was it misfortune,
Or was it luck,
The day we met?
Is it to be thankful,
Is it to be grateful,
Or is it to regret?
That day we didn't
Know of our
Impending rocky ride,
We didn't know
Of the turbulence
Or of our fragile sides.
Like a Rollercoaster
We went up and down,
Tasting displeasure and the sweet,
Being in passion and being in pain,
– laughing aloud in the street.

All this is the roll of the dice
And clichés mainly apart,
All things being considered,
      deep down,
I know you have a perfect heart.

Half-a-Sleep

I can't do small talk,
It bores me really shitless,
Conversations about the trivial
Can make me look really witless.

Give me lessons how to do it,
Talking fluently and how to keep,
But bloody well hurry up
             – I'm already half-a-sleep.

Visitor

The razor scythe and hidden
Face, a skeletal hand to grasp,
A knocking comes to the door
This is the one at last.
It is feared this shadow dark,
Its tallness overhead,
When the time is to be right
It will tell – be dead.
The staying option can not be,
Infinite cannot be sold,
When the figure comes to you,
You will exit when you are told.
But don't fear the visitor,
Its taking may be its giving,
It comes to show the way out,
An escape route for the living.

Folk

Poetry must be boring
This is what I assume,
When you mention it to folk
They promptly walk out the room.

Looking Back

Looking back I see a small boy climbing a tree,
A small boy laughing with a scar on his knee.
One blissfully unaware of the future to unfold,
A boy then fresh faced, not pleasing until told.

Looking back a thin slab, a clean piece of slate,
An arrogant reminder not carved with the date.
A young boy learning often not by his choice,
Fleetingly innocent with no depth in the voice.

Looking back at purity time removed without trace,
Back then no introspection in the eyes on the face.
Once a young sapling with eagerness to grow,
Unblemished like a pathway after falling snow.

Looking back and witnessing youths' full day,
No philosophy sliced here for the boy to say.
Once rawness and vigour and manners that lack,
Now staid and compliant and aged . . . looking back.

Sleeping

Don't write it off as purely negative
Even if this is how it seems,
When you go, so do your problems
        . . . if sleeping without dreams.

Push him over
(Don't)

Push him over,
Push him over the precipice.
Lean on him,
He is a rock,
He's a rock of blancmange.
He says he's been drinking
And doesn't feel too good.
He says he has some marginal
Physical discomfort
But an eternity of psychological
Disturbances that weigh down
On his soul.
He's confused,
He doesn't like changes or the
Great and many uncertainties.
He's an obsessive
And he wonders why he is
Telling you to write
This damn poem.
There's no reason to write it,
So don't.

Consideration

A core of fractured thoughts
Under a veil of well-adjustment.
The covert habit or
Self-confessed inclination
Enveloping dysfunctional psychology.

Temperance and abstinence.
An everyday vying,
An everyday struggle,
An everyday consideration.

Again

Cans of beer
You are
Personified beauty,
Created for the insane,
When I start feeling sober
You get in my mouth again.

Mending

Take the pills
Think good thoughts
Float along life's path,
Take the pills
Think good thoughts,
Give your mind a bath.
Bathe it in chemicals
One sort or the next,
Bathe it in chemicals
Until it's no longer vexed.
String it out, float it on
Let it doze and unbend,
Let it rest and let it chill
And let it finally mend.

Tender

Tender and pale,
Lips pout from usage lack,
Crystal eyes open wide,
Open centres staring back.
Golden hair to feel,
Running fingers through,
Passion and inexperience,
One becoming two.
The tactile red plastic sofa
On which we were intertwined,
Propped our youthful confidence
And surged our youthful minds.
Schoolgirl brash and bated
Likes this schoolboy's face,
Paring now to practice
And trying to keep the pace.
Enduring pale lips and tender
A baptism of spring had seen,
Tender moments were to have
And tender moments been.

Ticking Over

The allure of carbon monoxide,
Scenes generated like
Engines ticking over in the final act.
Six cans and limitless whisky,
Finding the escape route behind the
Garage door.
Escaping to the twilight world,
The final dream pipe and limitless sleep.
Little time for evaluation, just
Driving down the road and over the cliff.

Slightly Smiling

Lying still in your box, slightly smiling
Under grey satin, the people had observed
Your passing from what they know
To what they don't.
Transcending from the mortal plain,
You had flown like
Some liberated sweet spirit
From your earthly home.
There was a voice and laughter from
Your silent lips, drifting
In the air and settling
In the minds of the people stood.
Early recollections of your image and early
Photos of your being, fused with the final hours,
Imprinting indelibly in the mind.
You rested now in some other dimension.

For our lives together and for what you gave,
We say thanks and know we could not exceed
              . . . your every way.

Harder to Write

He's strung-out on anti-depressants,
His wife said to take them right now,
Because he has to stop being a 'Cuckoo'
And be an ordinary person somehow.

However, this detachment is not all bad,
He can't wait for his pill every night,
But on the downside it has to be stated,
     – the poetry can be harder to write.

It's no Fun being a Pet

It's no fun being a pet,
Your life's in a cage
And then to the vet.
You don't have a mate
Or sex on a plate,
You're just
Watered and fed
And then with a prod
From some silly sod,
They make you
Sit up and beg
Or dance or run,
And the mind
Becomes numb.
It's no fun being a pet.

The Mind a Tome

As the mind examines
The pages of the past,
Apparent damage
To some would exist,
But not healthy to dwell
On the previous events,
The mind moves on
And resists.

It resists the taunting
Of events now gone,
When maybe different
It could have well manifest,
These tortuous pages
Are well left alone,
And the tome
Well left to rest.

True Friends

Stroke the black resin,
Feel the pearlescent paintwork.
Dark as Raven plumes,
The form fulfils the master,
No one must come between us.
A window pane moves mechanically,
It reminds of the moving of feelings
When you are alone in the Tarmac
Wilderness.

Wheels rotate, sharp and smooth,
Blurring at the given speed.
Rear fin like marine excellence
Slices pieces of the atmosphere.
Down urban roads and
On country lanes,
We stop to hold and
Look and relish.
I am your life giver,
We depend on each other.
Separate not man
And the mechanical,
True friendships can be rare.

To be Free

Illness ravaged your body
And held you as its captive,
Never would you dramatise
Or seek pity from those around.
On drawing the final curtain
You left with your spirit
Whispering to those you love,
Free am I now, worry not,
With you I will always be.

Think of Me

On our parting and after you have cried,
Think not of me as leaving you
Think not of me as died.
Think of me as an opening flower,
Or as pastel summer colours at first hour.
Think of me as a young Swan or as a flying Dove,
Or as a burst of jewelled stars in the skies above.
Think of me as the mist or as the morning dew,
Or as an emerging Butterfly on its wings anew.

Cry not for me time after time,
                 nor as the day is long,
In all things I am with you,
                 and not to think as gone.

Illumination

A shaft of light
Will come to you
From the other side.
A shaft of light
Sensing an anguish,
Providing solace for
The inner disturbance
And pangs of loss.
The illumination of
A way forward,
A beacon of love
For sadness and grief.
Glowing and embracing,
A shaft of light
Manifest to you,
Touching your soul,
Will calm the disquiet
And return when it is
Time for you to join
Your forebears
Who wait . . . looking
Through heaven's gates.

6 am

Six chimes awake me
To the icy morn,
With heavy eyes and
Lightweight brain,
I stumble to the lawn.
Out of the shed a bike
Is led to the road
And then is mounted,
An icy skin is
Worn so thin as
The gradients are encountered.
Changing gears that bite
The heart, revolutions
Wear my heals,
Moving into second wind
Manpower is revealed.

Sorting

Possibly,
I was minding my own business,
Being nothing at all,
When suddenly I was born,
Was offered a dummy
And then began to crawl.
Walking and talking
And a bundle of fun,
But nothing revealed
As to why this had begun.
Where am I?
Why am I here?
What is this being me?
The older to become
The more puzzled would be.
OK, I came this way
This is the thought,
But which is the way out?
Hang on
And the rest will just sort.

On Physical Beauty in People

He hates physical beauty,
A green tinge it puts to his blood,
But he knows ugliness needs to
Exude from someone,
To make the others look good.
He hates physical beauty,
It stirs an inner calm,
Taunting animal feelings
And raising the alarm.
He hates physical beauty,
Its confidence gets under his skin,
There's little consolation with details
Like ugliness has beauty therein.
He hates physical beauty,
If he once had it, he wasn't aware,
Sometimes it's only on reflection,
You realise when it was there.
He hates physical beauty,
But takes comfort in knowing
The score,
Put many years on physical beauty
And it's not beautiful anymore.

Historic

If you're gone, what will a field
Of golden grain look like?
Will you feel the wind on your
Tombstone?
Will you feel the dry kisses
Of the living and see traces of your
Life in waterfalls and rainbows?
You are a snapshot in mankind's
History – you have been here,
That's your only credential.
On which part of the great cosmic
Interchange is your memory etched?
Collective history – you are a part of it,
But you are actually not significant
And will quickly fade to
Historic bollocks.

Rescue

Dry mouth, beer yesterday,
Copious, acid-reflux.
Rescue me from tonight
And its obsessive consumption.
Day moves on and the beast
Is released for the ceremony.
Cigarettes and quantities of
Strong beer pacify and aggravate.
Morning holds unpleasantries,
But the time to re-indulge
Will soon be here again.

And then Sleeps . . .

Take hold and push
For fortune
Like trying to win
A bear at a fair.
Sliding garments,
Pumping blood.
Sun rays through
Curtain fabric indulging,
Landscaped linen,
Rhythmic jewels, muted cries.
Cultured Homo sapien
With all his intellect
And technology
Can't hide his animal status,
Can't hide his biology,
And then sleeps . . .

Laying

Next time he'll be a woman,
They have innate sexual power,
They don't go bald or have pot bellies,
And live longer with each hour.

But then he'd have to work harder,
Kids and housework and more,
He couldn't lie all day on the sofa
Or get pissed and lie on the floor.

Outside

The outside belies
An inside frail,
The venom Red
Is inwardly pale.
An exterior stone-clad
But curtains gentle and soft,
The windows are barred
And so is the loft.
To cope with being scared to exist
The veneer is cool to the touch,
The outside can be in your face
But the insides are seeking a crutch.

Undignified

However dignified you are
You'll probably end undignified
With somebody wiping your arse.
However great you are
You'll probably end without greatness
In some arse-wiping farce.
So prepare for the humble end
Where privacy may expend
And status and honour are
Frugally less than sparse.

For the Bottle

Anaesthetise life,
Detach from the scene,
Addiction to follow,
Self-creating, serene.
Clouding an issue,
Loosens a tongue,
And braver in battle,
Will fight and not run.
This is for the bottle,
For its sip,
For its tender opening
Pressed on the lips.
In consumptive flow,
You're slipping the slide,
And the bottle
Has no respect,
And definitely not
The contents inside.

Emulation of the Egg-man

The vortex swirls and pulls,
The futility persists but the
Body clock ticks on and fights.
There is an insidious metamorphosis
That depresses the soul and fuels the
Furnace of self-erosion.
The emulation of the egg-man and the
Mexican hairless breed, combine in the
Hybrid to form the just recognisable.
Shape, shave, grow and cut,
But you will not escape.
The genetic legacy has no preparation
And gains no sympathy.
Follicle failures should carry a health
Warning: 'This condition can be fatal'.

Flesh-Hunter

That guy,
He's a flesh hunter
And proud to admit,
Only trouble is
When he goes
Hunting,
He usually comes
Back with Jack-shit.
He might as well
Forget it and give
Up the fight,
He can manage
Without his quarry
– he does every night.

Living with Submission

Hostilities are settled a little,
He's left with the taste
Of defeat and its
Disagreeable aura,
Dry and vice-diminished
Trying to work out
Who or what is the enemy.
Is it his interpretation
Of the situation that's
Distorted,
Or is it about her failings,
However minuscule?
It is impossible to loath
What you actually love,
That's the ambivalent
Confusion.
Submission can
Breed disinclination and retribution,
But can also engender peace
And generate acceptance.
Submission hurts.

Calculating

If we all meet him at the other side
Later on, when we have died,
Will God evaluate
Our infirmities and our faults?
Will he unlock our bolts?
Will he give us points for moral abundancy
And black marks for its redundancy?
Will he wield his great power
When calculating in his heavenly tower?
And will he assess our earthly path
The one on which we've walked
And the one which we've sat,
Or will he just give us a jolly good
Ticking-off and let it go at that?

(If I'm a bit late, hang on).

Fields

I would be in the time of youth
When never a thought came to crumbling hearts.
I walked in fields with my Dog,
Through pepper meadows and down near the mine.
Into a nearby stream I tossed a pebble,
And saw it land serene,
Its ripples kissing the ladened banks of grass.
Later a stagnant pool I saw which held
No concealment,
As I stumbled on its slopes to fall,
I felt saved by the eerie solitude,
The mothers of all creation watched,
Faintly crying for natures directions.
Unanswered questions spun in the conflict of a mind.
I sat down and saw Spiders spinning their webs,
Like Dewdrops they were at the mercy of the wind.

These Solitary Tones

Frosted planes
Crack beneath the feet,
Soft snowflakes
Powered by hard winds
Drive forwards,
Lashing the face.
These solitary tones are
Surrounded by the white
And the crisp.
Considering all existence
And wondering if it could
Have been spared,
I crush the snow
In the hand
And feel its cold
Pain kiss the fingers.
I blame not the elements,
As a matter of fact they
Can only be of comfort here
Amongst these solitary tones.

Devotion to Cats

That mate of yours,
The extrovert,
The one it's hard to talk to
Without feeling like walking away,
He likes Cats.
He's always on about them,
He says he's got one of his own.
He likes them that much
He's got Pussy-Hunter
Tattooed on his arm.
That's devotion.

Enfolding

Summer comes
With the freedom
To liberate the
Captives of the cold.
A new season with warm rains
And Damson petalled Roses
With thorns to cut fingers on.
A season of addiction to the morphine
In the capricious heat of England.
Edible Nasturtiums and gardeners
Frenzied attacks on plant life,
Lawnmowers and incessant car washing.

Seeking the illusion of good health,
Imperfect bodies flaunt themselves
With expanses of white irregular flesh,
Commanding attention from passers-by.
In the rear garden on a sun lounger,
The floating mind dreams on,
Euphoric and hovering,
Basking in a haven of sunglasses
And the enfolding heat.

Addiction

He's dealing with it,
He's focused on it.
He's no grandiose plans,
Just simple ones,
Like,
Getting through each day
One at a time.

Some day,
We'll just be photographs

You've already seen images,
Shoulders and a face,
Of those of us gone before
To that intangible place.

Once living flesh and blood,
Framed paper now since gone,
Walking ones that would interact,
Now silent looking on.

Preserved for some time at least
Memories of good health,
– waiting patiently for you to join
And sit with them on the shelf.

Drink This

Peeping out
Into the world
Having a look around,
Quickly to retract a head
At any given sound.
Don't feel weak at many a sign,
    – drink this you'll be fine.

Climbing out
Into the world
Walking now around,
Quickly to retract a head
At many things being found.
Foreboding not or fear thine,
    – drink this you'll be fine.

Tranquil Mind
(A broken lock)

In my time I have decided,
A tranquil mind
To evade,
Is suicide from the outset
This is my serenade.
Striving for this elusive
Device is a must,
Locate and find
Before you rust,
Before you finally mistrust.
Strive before the rot and the slide,
Before the sickness inside,
Before the end is in sight,
Before this very night.

A tranquil mind is never seen,
The sleeping never awoken,
Tranquillity is the key
But the lock is fucking broken.

Crazed

It's enough to make you barking,
All this thinking and larking,
About why we're here
And where we'll go.
Don't froth and feel crazed,
Or try clearing the haze,
Because maybe you'll never know.

Leave your mind alone, stop its debate,
Stop racking a head, or to create
A depression or sadness inside.
Accept the scene, accept the plot,
We're here like it or not,
Your only choice is to abide.

Hearts and Flowers
(Ending on a good note)

Forget ye depressive breath of death,
In rough seas there's land ahoy,
Keep your chin up on the highway,
Be ye positive and enjoy . . .
> . . . it's all hearts and flowers.

Notes for readers

These are 'one line' notes on a few of the poems. They are not essential because reading a poem is like looking at a painting, you take away or leave behind whatever you like. It's always about personal interpretation and therefore the supporting information surrounding a poem and its inception is far from crucial. Anyway, from a curiosity angle I've included here very brief details.

Snakes
Respect to one of natures greatest and often unjustly maligned animals.

From you
Indebted to parental figures. Mum for her sustaining support and Dad for his guidance and influence on my writings when I was young.

Ice
This was written when I was sixteen and holds a special place.

Privilege
When my thirteen-foot Burmese Python found a new home.

Gentle Death
From my ponderings in the early eighties.

Last Stop Dies
A youth on a bus trip – the first letter of each word in the title explains.

Introsurdity
This word is self-created and not in a dictionary. A diagnosis in the grip of alcohol.

Immovable
After collective discussion on inter-marital disputes.

Obviously Important
As a snake keeper, I had a realisation.

Consideration
On abstinence from alcohol.

Tender
We were two school kids who tasted the experience of togetherness.

Think of Me
As a comfort to the bereaved, this is probably the most poignant poem I have written to date.

And then Sleeps . . .
Space exploration, computers and telecommunications, but in some places no different from the beast of the field.

Tranquil Mind (A broken lock)
A search for the ever-elusive tranquil mind.

Hearts and Flowers (Ending on a good note)
Remember to keep your chin up.

Chronology

Dates in chronological order (inception of each poem).

1974 Ice.

1975 Last Stop Dies, Swans, The Warlock.

1976 6 am, These Solitary Tones, The Mind a Tome.

1977 The Angel on Golden Wings.

1978 Fields.

1982 Gentle Death.

1991 Push him over (Don't).

1993 Quell the Tide.

1994 Emulation of the Egg-man, Slightly Smiling, The Beast Devours, Ticking Over.

1996 Snakes.

1997 Sarcophagus, I Wrote this, Too Many.

1998 Swimming God's Pond, No Smoking in Heaven, On Physical Beauty in People, Should you tell your Babies? Looking Back, Still Some Life, Hearts and Flowers.

1999 From You, Tomorrow, Bruised Cross, Timepiece, You, She's Terrific, Calm Sea, Someone Said . . . , Beauty Cloaked, Voyages of Obsession, Cacti, Unsavoury, Treadmill, Sleeping, Rescue, And then Sleeps . . .

2000 The rest of the poems in this book are written in this year.

The author's quotes

He knows when he's been drinking too much,
he can feel something hard in front of his face,
                    – it's the floor.

To Mum and Dad, you brought me here,
            – but how long do I have to stay?

He looks at life through shit coloured
spectacles and cleans them regularly with beer.

To itself, the humble Goldfish is more
important than a president.

A can of beer is like a woman
            – only one tastes better.

If he wants to, he can stop drinking,
he did it the other night, he chained himself
to a radiator in the living room.

Like the gentle falling rains, the poet
touches and embraces the human spirit,
            – then he gets wrecked and acts
                    like a complete bastard.

119